Hedgehogs

and Other Insectivores

Concept and Product Development: Editorial Options, Inc.
Series Designer: Karen Donica
Book Author: Steven Otfinoski

For information on other World Book
products, visit us at our Web site at
http://www.worldbook.com

For information on sales to schools and
libraries in the United States, call 1-800-975-3250.

For information on sales to schools and
libraries in Canada, call 1-800-837-5365.

World Book, Inc.
233 N. Michigan Ave.
Chicago, IL 60601

Library of Congress Cataloging-in-Publication Data

Otfinoski, Steven.
    Hedgehogs and other insectivores / [book author, Steven Otfinoski].
        p. cm.—(World Book's animals of the world)
    Summary: Questions and answers explore the world of insectivores, with an emphasis
on hedgehogs.
    ISBN 0-7166-1208-9 — ISBN 0-7166-1200-3 (set)
    1. Hedgehogs—Juvenile literature. 2. Insectivora—Juvenile literature. [I. Hedgehogs—
Miscellanea. 2. Insectivores—Miscellanea. 3. Questions and answers.] I. World Book, Inc.
II. Title. III. Series.
    QL737.I53 O83 2000
    599.33—dc21
                                                                            00-021638

Printed in Singapore
1 2 3 4 5 6 7 8 9 05 04 03 02 01 00

World Book's Animals of the World

Hedgehogs
and Other Insectivores

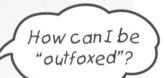

How can I be "outfoxed"?

World Book, Inc.
A Scott Fetzer Company
Chicago

Contents

What's my scream mean?

How can I be scared to death?

What is so great about being a big mouth?

What Is an Insectivore?

Mammals are divided into groups called orders. Each order is made up of animals that are closely related. Insectivore *(ihn SEHK tuh vawr)* is the name of an order of small, primitive mammals that eat mainly insects. There are about 400 kinds, or species, of insectivores.

Although they are primitive, insectivores are amazingly diverse in how they look and where they live. The hedgehog *(HEHJ hahg)* is one special kind of insectivore.

Hedgehog

Where in the World Do Insectivores Live?

Insectivores live almost everywhere. Shrews *(SHROOZ),* for example, live on every continent except Australia and Antarctica.

Hedgehogs live in Europe, Asia, Africa, and New Zealand. Moles live in North America, Europe, and Asia. Solenodons *(suh LEE nuh dahnz)* are insectivores that are found on only a few islands in the Caribbean *(KAR uh BEE uhn).* Tenrecs *(TEHN reks)* live on islands near the coast of Africa.

Some insectivores live only on land. Others spend much of their lives in or near water. Still others, like moles, live underground.

World Map

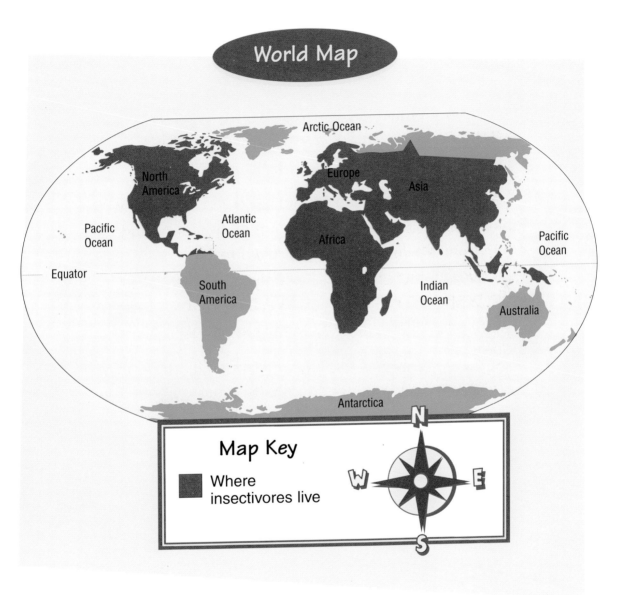

Arctic Ocean

North America

Europe

Asia

Atlantic Ocean

Pacific Ocean

Africa

Pacific Ocean

Equator

South America

Indian Ocean

Australia

Antarctica

Map Key

Where insectivores live

N

W   E

S

What Makes a Hedgehog a Hedgehog?

A hedgehog's most striking physical feature is its spines. These long, stiff, needlelike growths completely cover its back.

A hedgehog's spines are its main defense against predators. When a human or another animal attacks it, a hedgehog rolls itself into a tight ball. All its spines stick out in every direction. Most predators will take one look at this spiny ball and go away. They do not want to tangle with all those sharp spines!

Hedgehogs are small animals that grow about 9 inches (23 centimeters) long. They weigh around 1 1/2 pounds (650 grams). Hedgehogs have short legs, short ears, short tails, and long noses, which are called snouts. They use their snouts to hunt insects.

Hedgehog rolled into a ball

 11

When Can a Baby Hedgehog Care for Itself?

An adult hedgehog may be able to take care of itself, but a baby hedgehog is helpless. Its eyes and ears are closed at birth. It is fully dependent on its mother.

A baby hedgehog's first set of spines is soft and white. The spines fall out in the first two to three days of life. The next set of spines is darker and harder. After about two weeks these spines begin to fall out. Then a third, permanent set grows in. About the same time, the baby hedgehog's eyes and ears open.

By then, the hedgehog is about a month old and is able to leave its nest and follow its mother. Before much longer it will be ready to leave the nest for good.

Baby hedgehogs
with mother

What Do Hedgehogs Eat?

They eat lots of things. Hedgehogs feed mainly on insects, but they also eat snails, mice, birds, frogs, and lizards. Hedgehogs are one of the few mammals that attack and eat bees and wasps. The stings of these insects appear to have no effect on the hedgehogs.

Hedgehogs have even been known to eat poisonous snakes! The snake's fangs cannot penetrate the hedgehog's sharp spines and reach its skin. The hedgehog waits until the snake gets tired in its attempts to bite it. Then the hedgehog grabs the snake and breaks its backbone. Finally, the hedgehog eats the snake—poisonous glands and all!

Hedgehog feeding

What Do Hedgehogs Do When There Is No Food?

In winter, food is too scarce to meet energy needs of many animals. That's when hedgehogs go into a deep, sleeplike state called hibernation (HY *buhr NAY shuhn*). A hedgehog's heart rate and all its bodily functions slow down. It gets what little energy it needs from stored body fat. The hedgehog is the only insectivore that hibernates.

Hedgehogs that live in deserts and other dry regions sometimes cannot find food in the hottest, driest part of summer. They go to sleep then, too. This warm-weather sleeplike state is called estivation (EHS *tuh VAY shun*). During estivation the hedgehog does not need to sleep as long or as deeply as in hibernation.

 16

Hedgehog hibernating

Do Hedgehogs Really Spit on Themselves?

Yes, hedgehogs do spit on themselves, but nobody really knows why. Hedgehogs will lick a rock or a piece of wood to start the saliva flowing. Then they swing their heads back and forth, spitting freely. Hedgehogs use their tongues to coat their spines with the spit. This startling behavior may continue for twenty minutes.

Some animal experts have ideas about the spitting. Some say the saliva the hedgehog produces may drive away predators. Others believe it attracts hedgehogs during the mating season. Still others say the saliva works against parasites *(PAR uh syts)*—usually ticks, fleas, or small worms—that feed on a hedgehog's body.

Hedgehog spitting

How Do Hedgehogs Communicate?

Hedgehogs have several ways of expressing themselves. A content hedgehog will chirp, squeak, or whistle softly. When a hedgehog screams, it means it's in danger or in serious pain. When a hedgehog coughs, it does not mean it's sick. Rather, the hedgehog is sending out a warning to other animals to stay away from its territory or food source.

Watching hedgehogs in captivity shows that they also communicate with their spines. If there is a noise nearby, the hedgehog's spines will stand up straight in the direction of the disturbance. When it raises the spines on its forehead, the hedgehog is shocked or cautious. If a hedgehog trusts a person, it keeps its spines flat and even allows that person to pet it without being harmed.

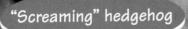
"Screaming" hedgehog

Do Hedgehogs Make Good Pets?

You may be surprised to know that the answer is yes. Hedgehogs can be tamed easily and can be as enjoyable as pets as dogs or cats. A pet hedgehog can even be trained to stand on its hind legs. You probably can find books in the library about the care and feeding of hedgehog pets.

Another good reason for having a pet hedgehog could be pest control. Hedgehogs can help keep houses and gardens free of bothersome insects and other pests. Unlike some pets, hedgehogs really earn their keep!

Pet hedgehog

Are There Moonrats on the Moon?

Despite their name, moonrats do not live on the moon, but in southeast Asia. Moonrats are relatives of hedgehogs and are one of the largest kinds of insectivores.

Moonrats look like large rats with black-and-white markings on their faces and tails. Unlike hedgehogs, moonrats have no spines to frighten off predators.

A moonrat's main defense when attacked is its mouth. When threatened, a moonrat stretches its mouth wide and shakes its head from side to side. This usually scares away an enemy.

Moonrat

Which Insectivores Can Be Fierce Fighters?

A moonrat's fierceness is mostly an act, but members of the shrew family can be real fighters.

Shrews are the smallest of the insectivores. They look like mice with long snouts. Shrews have tiny eyes and ears and short, dark hair. But don't be fooled by their size. Shrews attack, kill, and eat not only insects, worms, and snails, but also many larger animals, such as mice and frogs.

The short-tailed shrew, for example, has poison in its saliva. When it bites its prey, the saliva helps to weaken and kill the prey.

Short-tailed
shrew

Why Are Shrews Always Eating?

Shrews eat often because, although small, they burn up energy at a very fast rate. To keep their bodies fueled, they must eat nearly every waking moment. Many shrews need to consume about their own body weight each day to stay alive.

What if we had to eat that much? To give you an example, a child weighing 50 pounds (23 kilograms) would have to eat 200 hamburgers in one day!

Shrew eating
an insect

Why Do Shrews Have Short Lives?

Most small animals such as shrews have short life spans. Some scientists think the reason is that such animals need so much food. Burning all this food for energy may put too much stress on the bodies of the animals.

Shrews that live in captivity live only one or two years. Shrews in the wild face many more dangers that can shorten their lives even further. Animals such as owls, foxes, and weasels prey on them. Shrews also can be killed by parasites or diseases. Sometimes a loud noise such as thunder can scare a shrew to death!

Shrew as prey

What Are Some of the Smallest Mammals?

Shrews are among the smallest mammals. The pygmy shrew is the smallest mammal in North America. This shrew usually measures less than 3 inches (7.5 centimeters) from its nose to the tip of its tail. It weighs around 0.12 ounce (3.4 grams). That is less than a small coin weighs! Another shrew that size is Savi's pygmy shrew. It is the smallest mammal in Europe.

Newborn shrews are often smaller than a coffee bean. They also are blind and hairless, and they are completely dependent on their mothers.

Pygmy shrew and acorns

Which Shrew Has the Strongest Backbone?

The armored shrew of Africa is one of the largest and strongest shrews. It is also called the hero shrew for a good reason.

Unlike other mammals, its backbone, or spine, is made up of interlocking bones called vertebrae. The strength of this reinforced backbone is truly amazing. It has been reported that an armored shrew can support the weight of an adult human being atop its body.

The structure of the armored shrew's backbone is one-of-a-kind among vertebrates *(VUR tuh brihts),* or animals with backbones.

Spine Comparison of Same-Size Shrews

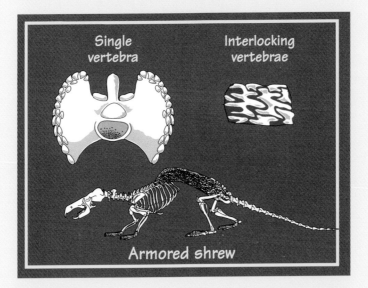

Single vertebra

Interlocking vertebrae

Armored shrew

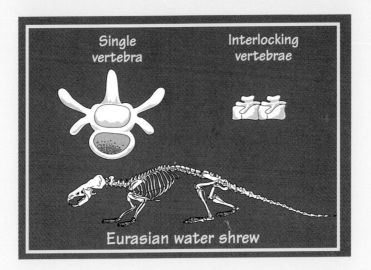

Single vertebra

Interlocking vertebrae

Eurasian water shrew

How Do Moles Get Around in the Dark?

Moles have tiny eyes covered by fur. They are almost completely blind. But moles manage to get around quite well in their dark world.

Unlike hedgehogs and shrews, moles spend almost their entire lives underground. They dig tunnels under the earth and live in them.

Their well-developed sense of touch makes up for their poor eyesight. Their sensitive whiskers and body hair help guide moles through the darkness. The tip of a mole's snout has tiny bumps that feel every object it comes in contact with. Moles also have excellent senses of smell and hearing.

Mole

Why Do Homeowners Dislike Moles?

Moles are expert diggers. And moles love to tunnel through lawns and gardens. They create molehills on the surface as they go. Moles dig some of their tunnels close to the surface where insects and worms can be found. Their digging cuts off root systems of grass and plants. One mole can ruin a lawn, a garden, or a flower bed.

The bodies of moles are built for digging. The large forelegs have flat, shovellike feet that turn outward. At the end of each foot are large, broad claws or nails, perfect for scooping out dirt. The heads and backsides are tapered, starting wide and getting narrow. This allows moles to move easily through the earth.

It is no wonder that many homeowners and gardeners dislike moles and set traps for them in their tunnels!

Molehills

What Is a Mole's Underground Home Like?

It's very dark as you might imagine. But if you could see, here is what you would find. At the center of a mole's network of tunnels is a nest. This is where it lives and sleeps. Some distance away from the main tunnels may be a room where a female mole cares for her young.

The tunnels branch out from the nest. About every four hours, a mole can complete a tour through the tunnels—looking for worms, spiders, and insect larvae *(LAHR vee)* to eat.

Mole tunnel

41

What Is a Mole's Favorite Meal?

Although they eat insects, moles prefer big, juicy earthworms. Moles like them so much that some moles store extra worms away for future meals in special storage chambers. A scientist uncovered one storage chamber containing 1,280 earthworms and some grubs. The total weight of the stored food was about 4.4 pounds (2 kilograms)!

Moles also like to feed on larger animals, such as lizards and mice. Like shrews, moles must eat an enormous amount of food every day to stay alive.

Mole eating
an earthworm

What Is Special About the Star-Nosed Mole?

The star-nosed mole is one of the strangest looking insectivores on the earth. It gets its name from its snout, which has 22 pink, tentaclelike feelers branching out from its tip. These special feelers help the mole find insects and other prey in its tunnels.

The star-nosed mole does not spend all its time underground, however. It builds its home near the shore of a brook or a pond or by a swamp. It is an excellent swimmer and often hunts for insects, fish, and shellfish on the water's bottom.

Star-nosed mole

Which Is the Largest Member of the Mole Family?

It is the water-loving Russian desman *(DEHS muhn).* This insectivore lives in southeastern Europe and central western Asia. Desmans are larger than moles, growing to lengths of 14 inches (36 centimeters) from nose to tail. They weigh about 6 ounces (170 grams).

The Russian desman uses its flattened tail and webbed feet to propel it through the water. When it needs air, it pokes its snout above the water's surface.

The desman is one of the few insectivores that does not live alone. Up to eight adult desmans may live together in an underground burrow.

Russian desman

Are Golden Moles Really Moles?

Sometimes a name can be misleading. Golden moles are not really members of the mole family. The main trait golden moles share with true moles is that both types of animals are suited to living underground.

Golden moles live in central and southern Africa. They get their name from their shiny, silky golden fur.

The most unusual member of this insectivore family is Grant's golden mole. While some true moles swim in water, Grant's golden mole— sometimes called a sand fish— "swims" in sand, digging tunnels as long as 145 feet (45 meters). The tunnels are not permanent because the sand is loose. New ones must be made all the time.

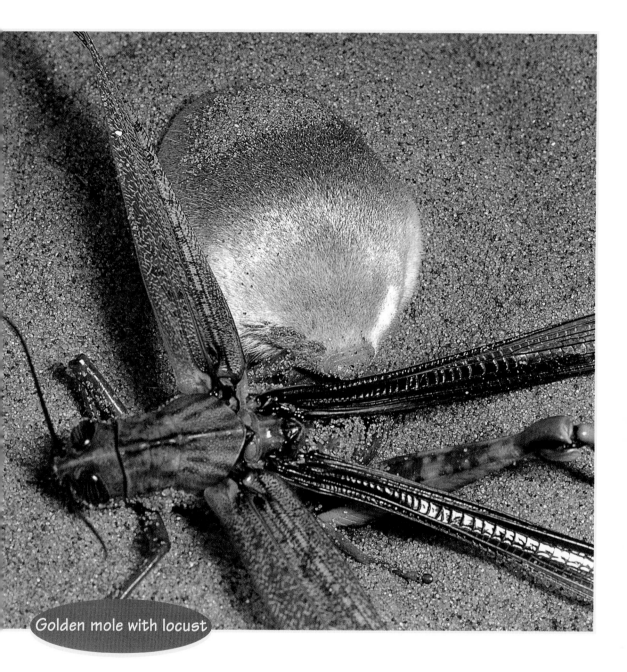

Golden mole with locust

Which Insectivores Are a Rare Find?

Members of the solenodon family are some of the rarest insectivores. They live only in remote parts of two Caribbean islands—Cuba and Hispaniola *(hihs puhn YOH luh)*. Hispaniola is divided into the countries of Haiti *(HAY tee)* and the Dominican Republic.

Solenodons are one of the largest types of insectivores. A solenodon can grow to nearly 2 feet (61 centimeters) in length and weigh around 1 1/2 pounds (680 grams). It resembles a rat but has a long, pointed snout and a hairless tail. The animal has sharp claws on its front feet that it uses to dig for insects in hollow logs.

Solenodon fossils found in North America reveal that these ancient animals lived there about 30 million years ago.

Haitian solendon

What Is That Clicking Sound?

It is a solenodon looking for a tasty meal. The clicking noises a solenodon makes create sound waves that echo. The way the echo bounces back to the solenodon helps it sense things in its path and find food. This complicated process is called echolocation *(ehk oh loh KAY shuhn).*

When the solenodon finds insects or small reptiles to eat, it bites its prey with sharp, grooved teeth. Poisonous saliva is released through the grooves into the wound, helping to kill the prey.

Cuban solenodon

Where Do Tenrecs Live?

These insectivores live on only a few islands off the eastern coast of Africa. Most tenrecs are found on Madagascar *(mad uh GAS kuhr),* where they have lived for millions of years.

Although they live in a small area, the tenrecs have adapted to several environments. Some tenrecs live in trees. Some live in water. Others live underground as moles do.

There are different kinds of tenrecs with different characteristics. The hedgehog tenrec has spines and a very short tail. The shrew tenrec has a long tail and soft fur.

Tenrec

Why Are Tenrecs Champion Mothers?

Female tenrecs, unlike most mammals, have lots of babies at one time. They can bear more than 10 young. The so-called tailless tenrec may have 25 or more young in one litter! That's more newborns than are born to any other mammal.

The newborns are naked and blind. Litters of tenrecs and individual animals develop at different rates. Usually, a few hours after birth, the newborn tenrecs can crawl like certain kinds of lizards. Within about 2 1/2 weeks, the babies are able to move around quickly in the nest. They begin to walk like adult tenrecs. Young tenrecs depend completely on their mother for food during the earliest weeks of their lives. The mother tenrec provides frequent and long feedings of her milk.

Later on, the baby tenrecs start to eat solid foods. The young tenrecs you see here were born in a zoo. They are sharing a helping of raw hamburger!

Litter of tenrecs

What Connects People and Insectivores?

While some insectivores, such as moles, can be a bother to people, most insectivores help people. They eat pests, especially insects that bite people and harm plants.

Hedgehogs in the wild are well liked enough now for people to accept them in their gardens and backyards. Once they were hunted as pests. Today the hedgehog is protected by laws in France, Germany, and many other countries in Europe. Some environmental protection groups even use the hedgehog as their symbol.

Hedgehogs, as mentioned earlier, make surprisingly good pets and can help control pests in gardens and in homes.

Pet hedgehog

Are Insectivores in Danger?

Not the little shrew you see here, but some insectivores are in danger of extinction. Hedgehogs are struck and killed in record numbers by cars in Europe. Many other hedgehogs die due to environmental poisons.

Several kinds of moonrats are losing much of their forest habitat. People are burning forestlands for agricultural use. The future of the Pyrenean *(pihr uh NEE uhn)* desman, a member of the mole family, is threatened by similar destruction.

Perhaps the most threatened insectivore is the solenodon. For many years, dogs and cats have been killing solenodons. Cuba and the Dominican Republic have passed laws to protect the solenodon. Many kinds of tenrecs are endangered, as well.

Common shrew

Insectivore Fun Facts

→ Savi's pygmy shrew, the smallest mammal in Europe, has a heart rate of 900 to 1,400 beats per minute.

→ Can anything "unlock" a rolled up hedgehog? A fox can. The fox rolls the spiny ball into a stream or a pond. The hedgehog unlocks itself to keep from drowning.

→ Some kinds of moles build a "fortress" around their nests, using the earth they removed from their tunnels.

→ Tenrecs are eaten as a tasty curry-type dish by the native peoples of Madagascar and other African islands. The animals are found by specially trained dogs.

→ A single hedgehog can have as many as 10,000 spines covering its body.

→ Baby white-toothed shrews stay close to their mother when on the move. Each baby will bite the fur of the one in front of it. The first one holds onto the mother. When the family moves, the shrews resemble a twisting snake.

Glossary

captivity The condition of being held in a place other than one's familiar environment. The opposite of "in the wild."

chambers Roomlike spaces.

dependent Relying on others for what is needed or wanted.

echo To send back or repeat the sound of something.

echolocation The process of locating distant or unseen objects by means of sound waves.

energy The power used to act or do something.

environmental Relating to one's physical surroundings, or environment.

estivation A sleeplike state during periods of warm weather.

fossils The remains or traces of an animal that lived long ago.

glands Organs that produce and discharge substances used by the body.

hibernation A sleeplike state during periods of cold weather.

larvae The newly hatched and wormlike offspring of insects.

mammal A warm-blooded animal that has hair and a backbone. Females produce milk to feed their young.

parasites Animals that live on or in another animal and feed from it.

penetrate To pass into or through.

permanent Lasting without end or change.

predator An animal that lives by hunting and killing other animals for food.

primitive Simple, not well developed.

prey An animal hunted and killed by other animals for food.

propel To move forward.

remote Located at a distance or out of the way.

saliva Colorless liquid produced by glands in the mouth.

Index

(**Boldface** indicates a photo, map, or illustration.)

Picture Acknowledgements: Front & Back Cover: © Hans Reinhard, Bruce Coleman Inc.; © Erwin & Peggy Bauer, Bruce Coleman Inc.;
© Daniel Heuclin, NHPA; © Leonard Lee Rue III, Photo Researchers; © N. Smythe, NAS Photo Researchers.

© Erwin & Peggy Bauer, Bruce Coleman Inc. 59; © S.C. Bisserot, Bruce Coleman Inc. 55; © Jane Burton, Bruce Coleman Collection 13;
© Jane Burton, Bruce Coleman Inc. 17, 19, 43, 61; © Stephen Dalton, Photo Researchers 3, 15; © Michael Fogden, Bruce Coleman
Inc.49; © J.A. Hancock, Photo Researchers 53; © John Hartley, NHPA 47; © Daniel Heuclin, NHPA 5, 33; © Dwight R. Kuhn 31;
© Dwight R. Kuhn, Bruce Coleman Inc. 45; © O.S.F., Animals Animals 11; © Rod Planck, Tom Stack & Associates 27, 29;
© Hans Reinhard, Bruce Coleman Inc. 7, 39; © Andy Rouse, NHPA 4, 21; © Leonard Lee Rue III, Photo Researchers 4, 37;
© Dr. Alexander Sliwa, Wuppertal Zoo 57; © N. Smythe/NAS from Photo Researchers 5, 25, 51; © Reneé Stockdale, Animals Animals
23; © Jean-Philippe Varin/Jacana from Photo Researchers 41.

Illustrations: WORLD BOOK illustration by Michael DiGiorgio 35; WORLD BOOK illustration by Patricia Stein 9, 62.